ENOUGH

— · IS · —

ENOUGH

JANICE MURRAY

NEWMAN SPRINGS PUBLISHING
320 Broad Street
Red Bank, NJ 07701

First originally published by Newman Springs Publishing 2018

ISBN 978-1-64096-165-4 (Paperback)
ISBN 978-1-64096-166-1 (Digital)

Printed in the United States of America

To my husband, grandchildren, mother, father (in loving memory), and family and friends.

Chapter 1

Where It All Started

MY NAME IS JANICE \Dzhenis\; I was born in Seale, Alabama, graduated from Chavala High School in 1982. I became pregnant in 1982 with a baby girl named Tabitha. When I got pregnant, I was eighteen years old, and I was still living with my parents, Miriam and Albert. I wasn't getting any help from Victor who was the father. Victor was in the military stationed in Korea. I did not hear from Victor for a while.

One day, he called out of the blue and said, "Do you know who this is?"

I said, "Yes, it's Victor."

He asked how the baby and I were.

I replied, "We're fine."

Victor stated, "You think I don't love you or care?"

I answered back, "You don't." The phone call conversation with Victor wasn't long. After hanging up with Victor, I knew I wasn't going to get any help from him. So I decided that I better start looking for a job. So I did.

I was working in Pine Mountain, Georgia, called Cagle's. It was a chicken plant. So time went by, I was still working at the plant. One day, I came home, and I showed my mother my swollen hand. My mother said I better rub them with alcohol so you can go back to work tomorrow. If you're from the South, people believe alcohol cured everything.

So I got up early the next morning around 4:00 a.m. to get ready. My ride picked me up every morning. At this time, I was still pregnant with Tabitha. While I was at work, I was on the assembly line watching the chicken come down the line. All of a sudden, I wasn't feeling well, so I told my supervisor then that I wasn't feeling well.

Then the next thing I knew, my supervisor was telling me I passed out, unaware that I had fainted. That day I went home, and my mother asked why I was home so early. I replied back to her and said that I fainted at work. After I passed out, I did not continue working at Cagle's. I stayed at home until it was time for me to have my baby. In 1983, I had my first child at the age of nineteen, which was a beautiful baby girl, at Cobb Memorial Park in Phenix City, Alabama.

My friend Sarah was there with me because I had to call her to take me to the hospital. The baby and I came home, and I was still living at my parents' house. As time went by, I decided to tell my mother I was moving out; my mother replied, "You're not moving out!"

I said, "I said, yes I am mother." I found my first apartment in Riverview in Phenix City, Alabama. My mother still did not believe me until the time came for me to start moving my things out.

Then it hit her, and mom said, "You are moving out."

I said, "Yes mom. I'll be moving to Riverview apartment."

I stayed in Riverview for about three months. I didn't like where I was living because it was a ghetto place. Neighbors always wanted to borrow sugar, eggs, etc. Whatever else, it did not matter. The same complex that I lived in, people had issues with me. But that wasn't the reason I moved out. I was brought up not to let people come in and out of our home. So I moved out of Riverview and found a much nicer apartment near Canterbury.

When I first moved there, my neighbor and I got along. But as time went by, my daughter would be playing, and I guess she would be too loud, and then the neighbor started to complain about the noise. If you have children in the house, it is going to be somewhat noisy. So she would complain to our landlord, and the landlord gave me an eviction notice. So here I go again looking for another place. My mom's friend had a house for rent, so I rented that house from her on Seale Road in Phenix City, Alabama. Finally, I had found the right home.

Chapter 2

The Journey in Germany

Now it's time for me to have some fun. So Robinson headed off to Germany. Soon after Robinson got settled into his assignment, I received a call from my husband saying, "Are you ready to come over?"

I said, "Yes."

Robinson said, "You and the kids, I have your tickets." I received our tickets in the mail. After a week or so, it was time for us to head out to Frankfurt airport in Germany. It was a long trip, but I must say traveling with two young kids went better than I thought. The plane ride was nice; we got to watch a movie and had dinner.

Finally, the plane had landed. My husband was there to pick us up. I forgot one important member of our family; my dog. His name was Bear. How could I forget Bear? So we all loaded up in the car, and Robinson took us to our new apartment. The apartment was very nice, and it was a quiet place to live. Although we had not received our own furniture, the apartment came with German furniture. If you know anything about their furniture, it is very low. It wasn't a very nice furniture, but we made do with what we had.

Finally, our furniture arrived. It took me about a week to get everything right. My husband and I signed the kids up for school. It was a very nice school. It was very close to our apartment. We walked the kids to school every morning and after I would go back home and clean up. And after that, I would be bored, but soon after, I met a friend named Chloe. We would walk on post to see what jobs was posted on the board; they didn't have anything.

So one day, we went on post to check the board. They had a posting about how to start your own home childcare business, so my friend Chloe said, "Dzhenis, we can do this. We could start our own day-care business."

At first, I wasn't sure, but Chloe said, "We can do it, I'll help you." So my friend talked me into it; we had to attend all the classes that were there. An inspector came out to check out our home day care. And the same day, the inspector gave me the okay, and I passed the inspection with flying colors. So I began to advertise my business, and my husband took a flyer to work. Some of his soldier friends became my clients. That's how I started to meet lots of my friends. Also, a friend that lived in my building became my client. Chloe would be a backup providers for me. We would be back up provider for each other, and we would take our kids out to the playground together and do activities together. This went on for about a year.

After a while, I just became bored in the house all the time with the kids. So I decided I'll put an application in day-care center, and I received a call from the director and asked me if I was still interested in a position, and I said yes. So I started working at the day care, met new friends (some not so great). I would get off of work and pick up the kids and go home and cook dinner and ask the kids how their day was. They would always say well. Tabitha and Marques were good kids. They never complained about anything. There wasn't much you can do in Germany. My husband and I would take the kids biking, shopping, and attending church. We had a great time at the church. We met great friends at church as well. Marques played the drums; Robinson, Tabitha, and I would sing. I liked the idea of us doing everything together. After church, we would come home and relax.

We would change our clothes, then we would start dinner. After, my husband and I would take the kids and the dog to the base where there was a full field of rabbits that would just hop. The children would love just seeing them leap with their long ears and fluffy fur. The next morning, the children would get up for school, and I would go to work at the day care. And my husband would already be gone. In the military, he would have to get up early. He would have to run and do physical training (PT). In Germany, you could not start your car if it was cold; you had to get into your car and just go.

Another thing about living in Germany would be nude beaches. Sometimes we would walk out of the apartment, and the German people would be naked and laid out in front of the deck. So we would have to tell our children to close their eyes. Germany had this thing called junking where if people have things they don't want, they would drop it off. Whatever you saw or like, "You could get it for yourself. There would be good stuff."

Our friends also lived in Germany, the friends. We went to their house for a weekend. They were stationed in another part of Germany. We packed up the children and the dog and headed to our friend's house. We stayed up late talking about old times because my husband and Gavin were friends. They met in Fort Benning, Georgia. That's how I met my husband; I lived in Seale, Alabama. My spouse was stationed at Fort Benning.

I'd never forget, there was a young lady that liked my husband a little too much. She would always try to get my husband all to herself. From the church, there was another building where things were kept.

She got him over there, and I told my husband, "I better not catch you around that woman again."

My husband said, "I don't care anything about that girl. She needs me to go over and get those books we need for Sunday school."

I told my husband, "Don't you see, this woman likes you. Mind you, she has a husband."

I would tell my husband, "When we get out of this car, you better not say a word to her. You better not hug her or shake her hand." God was still working with me, so that passed by. She knew I wasn't playing with her trying to hang around my husband; she got the message. Each Sunday, my husband would bring flowers for the visitors.

The visitors like the idea of getting a flower, and once a month, we would have casual Sunday. People loved the idea of dressing casually. The Bible says, "Come as you are." We had a mixture of people. White, black, and German, all were welcome. We once attended a church in Germany where everyone drinks from the same cup for communion. I never saw anything like it before. It shows that we were all as one.

Germany was a quiet place, not much to do. The kids and I would go to the playground a lot, and the family would go to this big open field where we would walk around and just watch the children play, and our dog, Bear, would just run around. We lived a quiet life, and that's the way we liked it. A newly married couple moved into our building; they had two boys. So I decided since they were just moving in, I would cook dinner for them.

When I was finished cooking, I knocked on the door and told them, "Since you are just getting things set up, I made dinner for you and your family." His wife thought that was very nice; then a friendship began when our husbands would be at work.

We would visit each other. We became good friends as well as our children; her children would come down and play with my kids and our dog. We would also go down to the laundry room together (which was in the basement). We would go together because it was scary. Especially at night, it would be very dark. So we would always go together for our safety because there was a door on the other side, and other people could come in. I met beautiful ladies in Germany; good friends are hard to come by. Germany was a beautiful place to live. But not enough to do for family and kids. So now, I must say good-bye to my friends and hello to Pottstown, Pennsylvania.

Chapter 3

Welcome to Pottstown, Pennsylvania

MY HUSBAND PACKED UP THE family and headed to Pottstown, Pennsylvania. In 1995, we arrived in Pottstown, not knowing where we were going to stay. My husband talked to his sister, and her boyfriend she said it would be okay that we could stay with her boyfriend and chill until we got our place. My children went to school in Pottstown because that's where we were planning to live. My mother-in-law would bring us back and forth from Reading to Pottstown so the kids would be able to go to school. This lasted about a month.

Finally, we have gotten our place. It wasn't the best house, but we did not have a job at the time. My husband's stepfather allowed us to live in one of his houses. We did not have to pay rent because that was my husband's stepfather. As I said before, I know it wasn't the best house, but God put a roof over our head. Everything was okay in the summertime, but when it came down to winter, it was a different story. It would be freezing in Pennsylvania, and the water pipes would freeze up. That means we would not have water.

So my husband knew this man that would always come over to unfreeze the water with a torch, and this went on for a long time. It would rain and snow, and the water would flood the basement. I never saw anything like this before because I'm from Alabama. This went on and on. One time, it was so cold; we did not have any oil to keep the house warm. Good thing, my husband's stepfather had just put in a new electric heater. That saved us from being cold and frozen to death. We had to stay in that one room and stay warm. I could remember my husband crying, saying, "I can't take care of my own family." We would tell him we are okay as long as we had each other.

The winter went on. I can remember when we got snow in, and my husband and my son had to dig us out. It was so bad; other neighbors had to help us. You weren't able to drive to the store because the snowstorm was so bad. My husband had to get kerosene oil to put into the heater. Our neighbors let us borrow heaters. So finally, winter was over.

My husband got a job at a warehouse in Pottstown, Pennsylvania. I was looking for work. I was working at a day care for three hours a day. Not even that many hours because the owner would let me go home early. When things would be slow, I would walk home because at this time, we only had one car. I didn't mind walking home because it was during the summer, and it wasn't far from my home. So I would come home from work, cook, do what I had to do, and wait for the children to come home from school.

We had a dog named Bear. You could always tell when the children are closer to home because Bear would bark, and when the children come into the house, Bear would jump on them and be happy. The children would also be glad to see Bear. I would ask about their day.

They would say they had a great day. They would change their clothes first. People that grew up in the South know that when you come home from school, you had to change your clothes before you do anything.

So once the children change their clothes, they would eat dinner. And after that, it was homework time, and the kids would play outside for a while then come in to get their bath and watch TV until 9:00 p.m. Then it's time for bed. I would get the children off to school, then I would head to work. My husband would already be up and gone.

So I was at work. I was taking down an old paper off the bulletin board and put new paper on the board. It was a plain paper that my group leader had put up. So when she walked in, she said to me, "I like the old paper."

I replied, "Okay, I could put the old paper back up."

She said *okay*. I knew she didn't like the old paper. You sometimes know when you're new coming from another city, people try to try you. So anyway, I was asked to stay late, so I did.

We served the kids lunch, and after lunch, it was nap time. So the lead teacher and I began to talk. I told her, "If you know it or not, we are going to be best friends." At the time, she did not believe me when I first started working. There was a lot of work that needs to be done to the day care. It was good to share your experience with others; sometimes, people don't want your help, I can understand.

That one time, I had to ride with the van driver. She was asking me personal questions. I told her I don't share my personal business with anyone. "You don't share your personal business, and I won't share mine." After that, we still would talk but never about our business. The lead teacher and I became good friends just like I said. We would call each other on the phone after work. We have been friends for ten-plus years.

Okay, I'm moving on to another job at the YMCA. Remember I told you I only worked for three hours, not even that sometimes. So I had to find something better to help my husband pay the bills. So I started working at the day care at the YMCA. My lead teacher and I did not get along. She would always tell me and another group leader what to do. She would not do anything.

So one day when the children was down for nap, I had a talk with her. I said that it wasn't fair that we do all the work and she does nothing. She began to tell me that she had been going through a lot because her brother had been sick. I said, "I'm sorry about your brother, but we are to work together." After that talk, we became good friends. I was in this group called "Unison for Christ." She actually drew the picture for our organization T-shirts. She was an artist, and the director that worked there asked me if I could take on teaching other teachers how to set up their room. I did not take the job, so I decided to seek another job, and I did.

I started working for a school district. I worked for them for several years, and I had my ups and downs there. Children were disrespectful. I could handle that. I really had a close relationship with most of the students. I would call this one girl every morning to make sure she would get up for school. I want her to succeed. So many people had given up on her, but I didn't. She was a very nice girl but didn't have anyone to push her. Sometimes when you have older parents, they don't have the energy. Not all older parents, some can run circles around you.

So she did meet up with my daughter. She asked my daughter to help her with her graduation project. My daughter helped her with the project. I can remember I had this boy in class. He did not know how to read, so he would always put his head down acting like he was asleep. It's not that he would be sleeping. It was that he would be ashamed that he couldn't read. He was in special education, so that made him feel bad. I would always tell him he can learn. "If you don't try, you will never know what you can do." I can remember one day when he asked if I could take him to the doctor, and I did.

He was messing with some girl and caught something. I can remember the nurse telling me that it was very nice of me to bring him. I said, "Yes, thank you." I would take him to look for a job. All the things my children had that other children didn't, just for someone to care about them. This student would sell candy for my organization. When this student graduated, he moved back to Florida. Until this day, I still wonder, *Did he make it? Did he become a man? Did he succeed in life? I hope so.*

On to the next student. I have helped children who didn't have money for lunch. They would ask me, "Mrs. Dzhenis, I don't have any money for lunch." If anyone knows anything about living in the South, we do not like to see anyone go hungry. The first thing we ask when someone comes to our home is *can I get you anything?* That's part of what I was taught.

I can remember a student that I became very close to; she was a young lady that came from a low-income family. She had other sisters and brothers. I would look out for her at school. She became my son's girlfriend. Not only that, she had a baby with my son. My son was fourteen years old when he had his first child.

She was a little older than my son. She would come over and chill with him, and I would see her at school all the time. I would write a note for her if she would be late for class. I work downstairs whenever the children would enter the front door to come in. "If you were late, I'll send you to the office or write a pass, depends on what I want to do."

One time, I could recall it was her birthday. Every class she would attend to, she had a gift ready for her. She was so happy and surprised that someone would take the time out of their day to care for her like that. Her mother had called me and said that I was right on time because she didn't have any money to get her anything. I said, "You're welcome. She is a good girl."

Not only did I send her gifts to her classrooms, when it was lunch, I had cake and balloons sent to her table. She said no one has ever done that for her before. All that day, she was a happy kid. I could recall my husband teaching her how to drive. After all, she was having my son's baby. So my husband began to teach her how to drive.

Then the day came when she had to take her test to get her license. She got them on the first try. After that, I began to let her drive one of our cars. One day, she was driving my daughter's car and something told me to go to her school, and I saw all these kids getting into the car. After that, she wasn't allowed to drive any of our cars.

She was still dear to my heart. One evening, my son's girlfriend was walking home, and this girl wanted to fight my son's girlfriend. I told my son's girlfriend to get into the car. "You don't have to fight."

She said, "Yes, I do."

And I said, "If you fight, I will stay with you to make sure no one will jump you." Now remember, I am a Southern belle. I never saw anything like this before where children fight on the street, so she and the girl began to fight. The girl gets the best of her. But she got some good punches too.

Someone called the police, so I told my son's girlfriend to get in the car, and she stayed with me that weekend. From fighting, she had a knot on her forehead. So the weekend, she was staying with me while I was working on her knot. When she came to school on Monday, she had no knot on her head. The girl whom she fought probably thought she would come to school with a knot on her head which she didn't.

I can remember Tabitha and my son's girlfriend was in the same class together, and they got into an argument which leads to a fight. Everyone knew that my son's girlfriend was a big girl, and my daughter was a little girl. So the teacher walked out, and then they began to fight which put a damper on their friendship.

After they had fought, time had passed, and she graduated from high school. We made our way talking to each other again. I was always like her protector/guardian angel in some way. Yeah, I know you want to know what she had. She had a boy. I kept him with me all of the time. My son and I went to the hospital after he was born.

Her mother was there, a happy time for me being a grandmother. My son was younger, as I said before, so he was still in school. I can remember the boys at school did not like Marques. They didn't like him because he had everything: all the branded clothing, was popular, always with girls, never had to walk home unless he wanted to.

Those boys didn't care for my son. My son was a nice young man. I taught him to always be respectful to everyone, but they just didn't like him. One day, my son and I was in the kitchen talking. He said to me, "Mom, can I move to Alabama?"

I said, "Why?"

He said, "Before these boys kill me, or I kill them, it was best if I move with my grandparents."

I said, "Marques, I told you those boys you hang around are not your friends." So I got on the phone and called my parents. I asked them, and they said yes. That was one of the hardest things I had to do—to let my son go. Marques and I were very close. It broke my heart to see my son go.

Until this day, I still cry as I'm writing this. I have always raised my own children until he was fifteen years old when he left me. All right, let me back up. These boys had came to my house to fight my son while I was at work.

My daughter called me while I was at work that all these boys were in the back alley waiting for Marques. My daughter was brave to come out of the house with a broom and told the boys, "You aren't going to jump my brother."

So I left work to come home to make sure they were okay. They were okay. I can remember, one day, my son was going to a club for kids. He was fourteen years old at that time. My husband and I took him to the club and dropped him off, and we told him what time we would pick him up because the club closed at 10:00 p.m. So I told my husband, "Let's leave early just in case something goes down, we would be there to protect our son."

My husband decided it was too early for us to go and pick him up. Marques came out of the club mad. I asked him what was wrong. He didn't want to tell me at that moment. Somedays had passed, and he told me that he had got jumped. I asked him where your friends were. He said they couldn't get to him. I was thinking they didn't want to get to him, not they couldn't get him. At that moment, my son knew these boys weren't his friends. I had told my son several times these boys were not his friends. "They only want to use you for what you got."

To get a ride to the movies because their parents never took them anywhere and also a ride to the club. They were never true friends. I can also remember it was on a Friday night, my son was out late. I didn't know where he was, so I got into my truck to look for him. So I drove around, I didn't see my son. So I kept driving around. I saw a group of kids that was hanging out. So I pulled up to them and asked them if they saw Marques.

One child replied, "He in a ditch." I got out of my car, and I asked him what he said. He did not reply again.

But one of the boys that was with him said, "Man, that Mrs. ... You don't talk to her like that." Many of the students knew me from working at the school. I had gained a lot of respect from many students.

When I had gotten home, Marques was there in the house. All the time when my children would be out, I would have to worry about them. All the time. Boys hated on my son like I said before. I've never seen anything like it. So the day came to send my son off to the airport. Marques did like Alabama. He said that the children were nicer there, and he liked living with his grandparents. Marques fitted right in with the children. Marques started going to school.

The bus would pick up Marques right in front of the house. As time passed by, Marques started to miss school. My mother and father owned two houses.

So Marques would go over to the other house and stay by himself which made him feel like he was a grown-up. Marques would start missing school more and more as time went by. I can remember getting a call from the principal stating that Marques had gotten into trouble at school. He got in trouble because he was talking back to the home room teacher. She wasn't in yet, so I waited for her arrival. So she came in and I said, "I told you, I will be there, though the principal thought that I wasn't going to come."

The principal was one of my old teachers when I was in school. So she decided not to suspend my son. She gave him two days of in-school detention. Thank God, I was a good kid when I was in school; she did it for me.

So as time went by, Marques started hanging out with the wrong people again but this time decided to drop out of school. I was disappointed in my son. I taught him that education is very important. I would call Marques and ask what he would be doing. He would always say nothing. He would be at other people's houses, hanging out, drinking, and just sitting around. I would call every day. "Marques you need to be looking for a job, doing something."

He would get a job, work a while, then quit so he can lay around the house and do nothing with girls. He is a ladies' man, tall, dark, and handsome. This routine went on for years. Every time my son asked me to start a business for him, I did that.

I started this business that you can pick up junk refrigerators, stoves, iron, all items that you could sell that were metal or iron. So the business took off right away. I bought him a truck, looked in the phone book, started calling apartment realtors' office. I would send out flyers, do fax, doing all of this from Pennsylvania. My son began to get phone calls and started working the business and had one of his friends working with him.

This lasted for a while actually until he went back doing what he was doing before. Hanging out with friends, not picking up the junk that he was supposed to. Businesses would call me saying that he didn't pick up the items.

I would call him, and he would be sleeping or just playing around. Soon after, he just stopped getting phone calls because he would never pick up the ones he was supposed to. So I gave up after that. I told him, "I can't make you work. You have to want it yourself." I would receive phone calls from Marques's friends saying that he was locked up.

The common thing he would get locked up for was not paying child support. Then I would have to go to Western Union to send the money for him. And there was one other time, he got arrested at the Civil Center. He got stopped by the police by having open alcohol in his car.

The boy that was with him told the police officer, "It wasn't Marques's alcohol, but it belongs to me." The cop didn't care because it was his car. I could not get him out that day because it was a Friday. I had to wait until Monday. Before he got arrested, he just left his grandma's eightieth birthday party and got locked up.

I could not sleep at all that night. I got up early Monday morning ready for his girlfriend to pick me up, and I went to bail him out. So many times, I received phone calls about my son being locked up, especially the ones for not paying child support. I thought at one time, I was going to lose my mind.

Some time had passed, and he got an apartment with his first cousin. That didn't work out then got an apartment with another first cousin. They would call me for money to pay the light bill, pay rent. You know, being a mother, you try to help your children if you can, so I did. This went on for years, but I finally got a break.

My son grew up, had held a job for three years. Currently has three beautiful children. He isn't married yet though. I forgot to tell you. He did go to night school to get his GED and his CDL. He became a great man and a dad. Yes, he does live in Alabama. He only came back to Pottstown maybe twice, never to return. Enough about my son Marques, it is time to move on to my daughter.

Chapter 4

The Introduction of Tabitha

MY DAUGHTER BECAME PREGNANT AT the age of seventeen. She gave birth to a beautiful baby girl who she named Raelyn. She was a beautiful baby. I'm not saying this because she was my grandbaby.

When my daughter was released from the hospital, I went to pick her up and brought her home and took care of her and the baby. Raelyn was a good baby, didn't cry much, only when she would want a bottle.

She slept well at nighttime. Time had passed, and I guess about three months, Tabitha would be on her phone or just be doing nothing. Sometimes the baby would cry, and I would say, "Check on her." I started to realize that Tabitha had no interest in her baby. So I started taking care of her, bathing her, and feeding her.

She did not bond with her child. Time had gone past. Tabitha started hanging out with the wrong people. She learned how to catch the bus to Philadelphia. I wasn't aware that my daughter even knew how to catch the bus to Philly.

One thing about the streets, it will teach you things you don't need to know. Time went on, Tabitha would go to school and stay with this boy at his parents' house. Tabitha would call sometimes to let us know she was all right. I would always stay worried about her because she was in the rough part of Philadelphia.

So one day, she came home. She looked like the streets did beat her down. I would hold her and cry and say, "What have they done to you?" She would go to school but not much and right back out in the streets like it was calling her name. I did not know what she was doing to not keep her home. I could only imagine her hanging out with the wrong crowd of people. That's what had happened; She hung out with the wrong people.

She would come home when she felt like it. But this time, she stayed for a long time. So I had to call the school to tell them that my daughter had ran away. She became out of control. I had to call the police to let them know because I didn't want anything to fall back on me. Remember, she was only seventeen years old. She was supposed to be in school because you would get in trouble if you didn't send your kids to school.

So I had to cover myself by calling the police and the school to let them know. I can remember one time, she called us to come to Philadelphia to pick her up. It was the hardest part of the city. Never in a million years, I never thought I would have had a child like my daughter turned out the way she would be. So we picked her up and brought her home to get cleaned. I tell you, the street will do you in the wrong people, will have you act like them to be like them. The street doesn't care anything about you.

Anyhow, I talked with my daughter and asked her, "Why do you keep running away from home?" I would never get an answer. She finally (my daughter Tabitha) started hanging out with girls from Philly, just out of control. And would come home to see Raelyn whenever she felt like it. I can remember school being over, and Tabitha came home and got Raelyn and took her with her. It was getting late, there were no Tabitha nor Raelyn.

So I got into my car and started looking for them. I saw a girl I knew, and I asked her, "Have you seen Tabitha?"

And she said, "Yes, I saw her at the bus stop."

I said, "Do you know where Raelyn was?"

She said, "Yes, she was at Tabitha's friend's house."

I knew where her friend lived, right down the street from my house. I knocked on the door and asked the friend's mother where my grandbaby at. She said, "My daughter is babysitting her for Tabitha."

I said to her, "No one keeps my grandbaby but me." Tabitha's friend went to the back and got her, and I took her home and cleaned her up.

21

Anyone that knows me, if my grandkids goes anywhere with anyone, I will always clean the germs off them before I kiss them or play with them because there's no telling where they have been. So my daughter went on to Philly. I did not hear from her. Lost many sleepless nights. I had to go to work. I worked at the school my daughter was attending. I could not miss work, so my son would watch his niece for me so I could go to work.

I know what you must be thinking, *does he go to school?* Yes, he does, but I had to help my husband provide for the family. My son would say, "Mom, it's going to be all right." Tears would run down my face. She did get through school because when she was pregnant, I had teachers come to the house to help her with her work. They had a program from home. She did graduate and started working at McDonalds.

She started working at the age of fourteen. She was a hard worker. As time went on, she had gotten older, now eighteen years old. She started working at a home-care agency, became one of their best workers they had. Tabitha moved into her apartment with her boyfriend. So Tabitha and Raelyn moved out. I would still see Raelyn because my husband would pick her up when he got off of work and when I would come home from second shift. She would be awake on Fridays nights. She would hear the key in the door, and she would run downstairs and say, "Hi, Grandma!" and give a hug. Then we would go upstairs while I would be getting my shower, and she would be in the other room watching television until I get finished getting my shower. And we would stay up for a while just talking and watching television because we wouldn't want to disturb papa because he would be asleep.

Friday night would be the only night she could wait up for me. This went on for two years. Raelyn would greet me every Friday with a big smile and a big hug. Now Tabitha had moved out with her boy-friend. I could recall, my husband went to pick Raelyn up, and she was in the house by herself. My husband was so upset to see that she was in the apartment alone, so my husband took Raelyn into the car. And finally Tabitha came toward the apartment, and my husband said to her, "Where is Raelyn?"

She said, "In the apartment."

My husband said, "No, she is not."

Tabitha replied, "Yes, she is."

Finally, husband said, "I have Raelyn, but you should never leave her in the apartment by herself."

Tabitha said, "I just went around the corner."

My husband said, "I don't care. Anyone could have come in and took her."

So my husband and Raelyn got into the car. Each morning, we would have the same routine. My husband would drop her off in the morning and bring her back in the afternoon when he got off work. I could recall, I went to the apartment to see Raelyn. They were in the room, my daughter and her boyfriend still sleeping in the late afternoon, and I went to the other room to see where Raelyn, and she was sleeping in the room with two other boys in the same room she was in.

Something could have happened. I got my grandbaby up and brought her to my house and have her bathe, wash her hair. My daughter never thinks that something could happen. So I fed her, and she was glad to be with grandma playing.

My husband would rush to do his pick up so he could pick up Raelyn. This went on for a long period of time. So my daughter moved closer to us, and I was able to see Raelyn every day. I could recall, I just stopped by to see Raelyn, and she was outside playing with other kids. I asked Raelyn, "Where's your mother?"

And she said, "In the house with some man."

I told her to tell her mother you're going with me. Raelyn would tell me that she had to use the bathroom and the door was locked. You can imagine what was going on.

Some things are kept well enough alone, and I'll just leave that where it is. Now my daughter, Tabitha, had moved across the street from us. I could see Raelyn every day. She was ready to go to Grandma's house, and Tabitha said that Raelyn took an object and hit her mother upside her head. Then Tabitha got up and brought Raelyn to my house. I met Raelyn down the street and brought her to my house.

My daughter, Tabitha, moved a lot from one apartment to another. She wasn't a very neat person. I would come over and clean the apartment. I would come back two days later, and the whole place would be back nasty. Raelyn finally had to live with me and her grandpop because Tabitha's mind was not on raising a child. The street had her mind and boys. Remember, she was young when she had her first child. She would always be in the street. I could not keep her out of those streets. I would give her a whopping, and I would punish her and that would not do anything. It was like the street was calling her name, and she had to go.

Chapter 5

The Same Old

TABITHA HAS HAD HER SECOND child Tia. Nothing much changed, the same old things but with a different man. She was still in the street, but this time, she moved in with Tia's dad, Harrison.

They lived together for a while. I could recall that I got a phone call from the police stating, "Do you have your car?

And I said, "Yes, I do." I had forgotten that I had gotten my daughter, Tabitha, a car in my name. While Tabitha was asleep, he stole the car, and while the police was chasing him, he ran into several cars. Now back to the police, I said I have all of my cars out there. It was just that her boyfriend had stolen her car. They want me to press charges against him, but I didn't.

Tabitha's boyfriend went to prison for a while for selling drugs. Tabitha was always attracted to bad boys. I can't understand why because my husband would get up every morning and go to his job, so I knew she understood a good man from a bad man, and you don't choose those kind of men to be in your life.

Finally Tabitha's boyfriend got out of prison, and when Tabitha's boyfriend got out of prison, I started to keep my second grandchild. Being a mother was not on her mind. You can guess what was on her mind. Leave well enough alone, moving on.

Harrison went to Michigan to visit his uncle. While he was there, someone called the police and said that he had a gun. Harrison got arrested and stayed a couple months behind bars. When he got released, he came to see his daughter. He is a great father and tries to do the right thing. He was in and out prison, but now he has a job.

But I pray and hope. I pray that he stays on track and on a straight path. Now that Harrison and Tabitha went their own way, my daughter, Tabitha, met this man named Brady that was also a drug dealer, and she got pregnant by him also.

He was a handsome baby boy named Brandon. Down the line, I found out that Brandon's dad was beating on Tabitha. Every time Tabitha would come over to my house, she would be in a rush. I never knew why she had to rush, and once, she came over. She had a scratch on her arm, and I asked her how she get those scratches. She said her cat did it. She did have a cat at the time. I could recall calling her, she did not answer the phone, and time had passed. It was getting late.

So finally one of her friends had called and told me that her boyfriend had knocked her out cold. That was why I could not get in touch with her. So when Tabitha did call, I asked her about what her friend had said. Tabitha said it wasn't true. Her friend was lying because her friend had asked her to take her somewhere, and she didn't. So that's why her friend called and told that lie.

I could recall once, I went over to check on Brandon, and there were a lot of people in the house drinking and smoking. Brady also sold drugs. I went to the back and got my grandson and brought him home with me, and I called my daughter to tell her that these people were in her apartment.

She called her boyfriend and stated that she told him not to have people around her baby when she is not there. I could recall, Brady was still beating on Tabitha. I received a late night call one night, and it was my daughter, Tabitha, screaming saying that Brady is trying to fight her. So my husband and I went over there to see what was going on.

I grabbed my bat, and we arrived there. He was in that back, and Tabitha was in the living room. I asked her if she was alright, and she said yes. I asked to look at her back to see if he had put his hands on her or beat her, but there were no mark or bruises. So I went to the back where Brady was, and I told him if he put his hands on my daughter, I was going to call the police. Never got to say these words.

That was when my daughter told me if I go back there starting something that she would call the police on me her mother. After that statement, I was through with the whole situation. But I did take Brandon, and he lived with me and his grandfather. I told Tabitha that she can do what she wants, but Brandon will not be coming back until she gets her life together. I could recall, she called me and said that she and Brady was over. I didn't believe her.

My daughter, Tabitha, always lied for her boyfriends. At this time now, I have three of her children by three different men. So the kids and I decided that we would go over to her apartment just to see how she was doing. The apartment was very small, so we all sat in the living room. And I looked to the left of me, and there was a pair of men's boots. I asked her, "Whose boots were these?" I can't quite remember what she said. But I knew they were Brady's boots. So I said, "What is this room?" She said it was the bathroom.

So I got up and opened the door and true enough, Brady was in the bathroom hiding in the tub behind the shower curtains. I told the kids, "Let's go." And I told Tabitha that I was through with her. I can remember that telling this lady that I would talk to every now and then. She stopped by my house, and I was telling her that I am tired of Brady putting his hands on my daughter. I said God can handle him better than I can. I can remember at that time, Tabitha came to my house with one of her eyes closed.

I knew Brady had done it. She said she was in a car accident. I knew that wasn't true. A steering wheel could not have done that that had beaten her eye closed. I told Tabitha Brady did it. She said, "No, he didn't."

I said, "Yes, he did." And then she went out the door. I could recall, I needed Tabitha to do some paperwork. And she said, "I'm in a rush. I have to go."

I said to Tabitha, "I always do what you need me to do." Let me back up. Brady got locked up for a while. I was glad that way. She didn't have to get a beating for a while.

27

He was locked up, but she stayed in touch with him. She would go and visit him, and when he got out, things went just the same, went back beating on Tabitha. We as mothers need to know the signs when our child is being beaten on. I didn't know until about a year that my daughter was being beaten often, until one of her friends told me. I called Tabitha and told her if she doesn't leave Brady alone, I wasn't going to be there for her anymore. Then I thought about it. That wasn't the right thing to say. She didn't know how to get out of it. So I called Tabitha back and said that wasn't the right of me to do that.

"You will make up your own mind." I could recall, Tabitha was living with me and took Brady with her and didn't come home that night. She moved all her stuff out of her apartment. But Brandon was still living there, nothing in the apartment. Tabitha had stayed a night with Brandon, and Brady was sleeping on a cold floor. I found this out by one of her friends, so Tabitha got another apartment and moved Brady right on with her. She didn't take Brandon because I told her she wasn't going to endanger his life.

But she can do whatever she wants. I got tired of everything and turned it over to God, and when I did that, everything was in God's hands. I received a call from Tabitha's friend and said that Tabitha came home from work, and Brady had hung himself. She tried to take him down, but he was a tall man, and Tabitha was a tiny and short lady. So my husband got out of bed in the middle of the night to be with Tabitha. She was crying, and finally my husband returned home with Tabitha. And Tabitha then said, "Now you're satisfied?"

I said, "No, but we will get through this together." I did feel relief for my daughter knowing that she will never be beaten again by this man.

Brady had a hard life, in and out of prison; he did not know how to love because he was never loved. Tabitha raised money for his funeral. Brady wasn't in any insurance. So Tabitha and her friends would have something for a whole week to raise money for his funeral. Tabitha raised the money and had the funeral. They had T-shirts made with his son Brandon's picture on it. Brandon was a baby when his dad decided to take his life.

Chapter 6

Another Mistake

TABITHA MOVED ON AND HAD met another drug dealer. His name was Harry. She got pregnant with her fourth child. She was a beautiful baby girl named Janese. I can remember babysitting my granddaughter while Tabitha would be at work, and Tabitha would come and pick Janese up.

When she got off of work one day, Janese knew she would be the only one going with her mother. The other children are older now, her other brother and sisters. So one night, Janese decided she wasn't going home with her mother. Janese looked at me and said she wasn't going home with her mother anymore, and she didn't. She stayed with us.

When Janese was born, I would go over to Tabitha's house to check on my daughter and granddaughter. The house would be filthy. I would go over there and clean it up and give Janese a bath and wash their clothes. I would come home the next day and the same thing: clean the house, wash dishes and clothes, and dust, the things a mother should do. But my daughter never ever hardly kept the house clean.

People would be over all the time, and at the time, Harry had gotten another girl pregnant at the same time my daughter was pregnant. She would walk by my daughter's house. I guess to see if she would see Harry.

So one day, the girl walked by my daughter's house again. But this time, they exchanged words. My daughter stepped down off the porch, and they got into a fight. My daughter has had her baby, but the girl she faulted was pregnant still. So my daughter, Tabitha, faulted a pregnant woman. The police was called, and they arrested Tabitha.

Harry called me and said the police took Tabitha in because she had faulted his girlfriend. So I went down the police station and said, "I'm here to bail her out." They said that they don't take money at their police station.

The police looked at me and asked me, "You can bail her out?"

I said, "Yes, how much?" My bank is across the street. The bank was closed, but I had my ATM card to get her out.

I believed it was about $700.00, so I got the money from the ATM and gave it to Tabitha's boyfriend Harry who is a drug dealer but did not have any money to get her out. So anyways, I gave him the money and went and bailed Tabitha out.

So Harry followed the police while they transported Tabitha to the prison. I told Harry to call me when they let her out. I waited up all night waiting for Harry to call me. It was about one o'clock in the morning before I got the phone call saying that he had bailed Tabitha out. This would not be the first time Tabitha goes to jail nor her last. I could recall, Tabitha had a warrant in Reading, Pennsylvania.

The police came to my house and asked, "Does a Tabitha live here?"

I said, "No, she doesn't live here." The police said that she has this address.

I said, "I don't care what address she has. She doesn't live here. My daughter and I do not talk, and if her sister sees her, I'll give her number and have Tabitha to call you." Tabitha doesn't have a sister. Soon as the police had come by looking for her because she had an outstanding ticket, she said okay. So she would go to work in different cars, trying not being noticed because the police knew what kind of car she was driving.

After she knew she had a warrant on her, she stopped coming by to see the kids. I would meet her at the hospital and bring the children in the parking lot for her to see them for a minute. My husband would always say, "The police could be watching you."

I said, "No police watching, nobody." So finally, it all came to an end. The cop did get Tabitha. It was up in Reading, Pennsylvania. I received a call from her drug-dealer boyfriend Harry. Once again, he didn't have any money to bail her out, so Harry and I went to Reading so I can bail her out. The bail was over a thousand dollars. But I had it. I went to the bank and got the money out and headed to Reading to bail her out.

After all that, we got there. Tabitha was there in handcuffs, and I was talking to her and said, "Mom, you can't talk to me." I said why. She said, "Because I've been arrested."

I said, "Okay, I didn't know."

So then the judge said, "Who here to bail her out?"

I said, "I am."

The judge had to run my name. I said to the judge, "I have never been arrested." I guess if I had a warrant, I would have been locked up just like Tabitha. Thank God, I haven't been arrested nor ever had a warrant.

So anyhow, he ran my name and found out there wasn't anything on me. So I paid the thousand dollars and got Tabitha out of her mess and took her to her home and Harry her boyfriend. But the word was on the street that Harry had bailed her out.

You know that old saying, Harry didn't have a pot to pee in or a window to throw it out. Once again, she would always lie for her boyfriends.

Here we go again. Tabitha was in the car with Harry, and they were, by the police, found drug and gun in the car. They arrested Harry and Tabitha. Harry told the police that drug belonged to him, but Tabitha took the wrap for the gun. Tabitha took the case for Harry because Harry had a case already pending. Tabitha had gotten probation, but Harry served about three years in prison. Tabitha could have done time in prison.

But she was dented because she had a great lawyer that she only had to do probation for three years. Before Harry had gotten arrested, he had money saved up in case the police would catch him, had his lawyer ready and lined up. He had told Tabitha he had done the same for her. As time went by, Tabitha found out he had no money saved up for her.

So me and a friend went to her house and sold the big-screen TV. Harry loved expensive things. Whatever had a receipt, we took it back to the store and got money. All we could not find receipt for, we pawned the rest. All the money we had, we put it down for a lawyer for her. Tabitha never had good taste when it came down to men. She was attracted to bad boys. Here we go again, the cops are looking for Tabitha again, another warrant on Tabitha, so I received a call that Tabitha had been arrested.

I received a call that morning from Tabitha's friend that everything had been worked out, not for me to worry because Tabitha had a friend that works for the judge that took care of all the paperwork to send to the judge she had to appear before. The judge that Tabitha's friend work for took care of everything.

The judge had called everything in, so once Tabitha turned herself in, then the process began. She was arrested, and her friend called me to tell me to head down to the police station where they had Tabitha held. So I arrived at the police station and asked them if they have a Tabitha, and they said yes. And I replied, "For what?" For outstanding tickets.

So finally, they brought Tabitha out to go before the judge. The courthouse and the police station was across the street from each other. So I walked ahead of them and had a seat in the waiting room until they brought Tabitha in. Finally, the judge called Tabitha's name. The police began to explain to the judge. "This is Tabitha. She has been on the run, and this morning, she turned herself in."

And the judge asked, "How long has she been out there?"

The officer said, "Three weeks."

The judge said, "She been out there. All that time if she had not turned herself in, she would still be out there." The judge said Tabitha had an unsecured bond and told the officer to take off the handcuff and get their shit together, and they have to let Tabitha go.

I knew before I got there, Tabitha would be released because the other judge took care of everything for Tabitha before she even turned herself in. The friend of Tabitha told the judge that she worked for that Tabitha had three children and would not be able to pay for bail. And that's how Tabitha ended up with an unsecured bond. So the officer took Tabitha to the window to complete the paperwork so she could be released. Tabitha and I looked at each other and laughed. We knew the deal before Tabitha turned herself in. I wish you could have seen the look on that cop's face. It had turned red.

The officer could not believe she turned herself in less than an hour, being held, and walked out the door a free woman. Tabitha and I knew she would be free because that morning, I received a call telling me how everything would be going down, and it went down just as what Tabitha's friend explained to me.

Tabitha would walk in and walk out. It was good to have friends that know people in high places. I thought, you only see this kind of thing in a movie. Tabitha and I could not stop laughing after the officer had let her go. The officer was confused about the whole thing, but Tabitha and I wasn't. One thing about Tabitha, she knows a lot of people. Tabitha knows how to work on you and get what she wants. It means Tabitha knows how to get what she wants and need out of you. After that, Tabitha hadn't been in any more trouble.

Tabitha never did serve any time in prison because I would go and bail her out. She would get off meaning her lawyer got her off the gun charges that she took for her boyfriend, only walked away with three years of probation. I wish I could say the same for Harry, but he did three years or more in prison and then was released and been out for a year or less. He got back on the streets doing the same thing that locked him up in the first place—drugs. Harry decided to sell drugs to one of his customers. She was a lady. Well, when he sold the drugs to her, she died. Harry was charged with murder.

The lady had cameras, and they stated that he was the last person to see her. So Harry went to prison waiting to go to trial.

Chapter 7

One After Another

So my daughter went to the next boyfriend. You should know the routine by now, right? You're right, another drug dealer. She is now on her fifth child, a baby boy. Jay was born a preemie and stayed in the hospital at least a month or more. My daughter went to visit Jay all the time, and the other kids would go and visit Jay.

Tiny little baby had tubes connected to him. He was very tiny. Jay finally got to come home. My daughter had her own apartment; I would go over to clean her apartment and visit Jay. She had to breastfeed the baby. He was still so tiny. Some months have passed by, and Jay is now living with me. Tabitha had no interest in raising neither her child nor any of her other children. But before that, I could recall not hearing from Tabitha in a while, so I called to check on her.

She was sick every time she would get pregnant. She would get sick. She would vomit with each child she had. So one time, I can remember while she was pregnant with one of the kids, she was throwing up, and I said, "Try this Pepsi. It might help. It always helped my stomach." But anyways, let's get back.

Tabitha had not called me, so I called her and asked how she was doing. She said, "I'm sick."

I replied and said, "Is Winston taking care of you?

She said yes, but I knew in my spirit that that wasn't the truth. So I got the other children, and we went over to check on her. My daughter, Tabitha, did not know if she was going or coming. In other words, she was very sick. So I got her and brought Tabitha to my house.

I got her back to her good health. Once I got her back on her feet, she went back home still carrying the baby. Few days later, Tabitha got sick again. This time, she had to go to the hospital. I was out, and I saw Winston driving my daughter Tabitha's car with other guys in the car with him. So I called Tabitha and asked her, "Why was Winston driving the car?" She said he had to pick up some house shoes and housecoat from the store.

So okay I let that slide. I went to see Tabitha and sat with her for a while because I had to pick the children up from school. Now Tabitha is out of the hospital, back in her apartment still pregnant and still getting sick. So that day, I just dropped by like I do all the time. She didn't call much. The kids and I would drop by when we want to. Tabitha was sick again. I brought her to my house and built her back up like I always do. She would get well and go back home. No Winston around out and about, just riding around in my car that I bought for my daughter with my name on it.

I asked Tabitha to call Winston and tell him, "He better bring my car back. If he don't, I'm going call the police and tell them he stole my car." But before I had gotten to Tabitha's apartment, the kids and I passed Winston on the road. Our eyes met, and he knew it was me. And when I arrived at my daughter Tabitha's apartment, I told her I passed Winston in the car, and he better bring my car back. So Tabitha called him and didn't seem to care about what she was saying. Winston did not bring the car right away. I told Winston, "I'm not Tabitha. I'm not the one to play with."

Finally, he brought the keys. I took the keys and brought them home until Tabitha had control of her life again. She would get sick until she doesn't know what really was going on with her. This had happened with all five children.

Until she wasn't able to take care of herself, my daughter had put me and her dad through a lot. I had always been by her side, always moving from one apartment to another. Her friends were nowhere to be found to help. I had moved my daughter out of apartments by myself.

While she would be at work, I could recall when she and I was moving out of her apartment from Brady, the one that used to abuse her. I was there to help her get out of there. Brady had come down the street talking junk.

I had another young man with me in case something went down. He would be there to put Brady in his place, so Tabitha and I kept going up and down the stairs. And we were loading things, and put it into the truck. And the young man was up in the apartment doing something else, "Dzhenis, how you doing?" He began to help us try to get Brady away from us. He did not leave.

Finally, I had to call someone else to come make him leave. Finally, Brady walked off with his friends and went with Tabitha, and I loaded up the truck and took it to a storage place until she got another apartment. And she did. After, Brady had killed himself.

She did get another apartment with Winston, another fool; I could recall that I had to go to Alabama because I had enough of the stress, so I decided it was time for me to visit my mother in Alabama.

I was tired—had to protect my grandchildren, had to protect my daughter from the wrong men she had chosen for her life, had to take care of my grandchildren being around wrong people. After a while, it could take a toll on you, and believe me, it did. I went to visit my mom for a week. I had a lot to think about.

Why did my daughter become this person? Everything that would happen would always be my fault. My daughter and I never had a good relationship as she have gotten older. She was a beautiful girl when she was younger. The streets taught her how to be mean, had no respect for herself or for others. She loved the streets more than she loved herself or her kids and would always give all her attention to her boyfriends.

I could recall when they would say, "I'm hungry, bring me this back." I could recall, she didn't move for her kids like that and wasn't eager to bond with them. Tabitha did not have a good relationship with any of her children because she always put the men first that was in her life. The children never came first. I could recall, Tabitha called the police on me because we have gotten into an argument. If she couldn't get her way with me, she would call the police on me and tell them I wouldn't let her have her children. The children had to go with her because she was their mother.

My daughter, Tabitha, never worries about the children when her boyfriends would be locked up. But when they got out, she would start trouble pulling them out of their home. Once the boyfriends would get out, that's when I knew I was going to catch hell. Tabitha wasn't a strong woman.

She always would do what her boyfriends would say. Pull the children out and didn't care about them crying, wanting me. As I could recall, this happened about two times. I told Tabitha if she ever pull my grandchildren out of their home again, there was going to be a problem.

Let me back up, Winston did go to jail. He got pulled over by the police with a gun in the car and some drugs. Winston served about three years in prison, so Winston got out in the summer time. When he had gotten out, him and Tabitha spent all their time together, didn't come to see the children, was doing their own thing, barely called. So one day, I called Tabitha about a loan I had gotten her.

I had borrowed money for her to start her business. Tabitha started her business. It started off slow, but it began to blossom and started making good money and was giving me money while her boyfriend was locked up. She would tell me about the clients she was getting and how much money she was getting for each client. I would go out on the streets to try and get her clients, tried to help like any mother would. Grandkids and I would go door to door and sell candy for her, trying to raise money because she needed a van. Tabitha stopped giving money, stopped calling, stopped coming by, stopped her checks from coming here. Her friend used to pick up the checks from my house. But when Winston got out, all of that stopped. She stopped sharing anything about her business.

I had to call Tabitha and told her she was going to pay me back the rest of the money she owed me. I told her, once everything starts taking off that I want six thousand dollars back. When I found out that Tabitha spent all the money, I had gotten a loan for six thousand dollars, and her friend was going in for the other six thousand dollars. Tabitha found out from one of her friend that worked at the bank that Tabitha's friend had taken her six thousand dollars out. She did not tell Tabitha what she had done. Tabitha called me and told me what her friend had done.

So I told Tabitha to call the bank and pretend she was me and get six thousand dollars more. She needed twelve thousand dollars in all. She only had six thousand dollars once her friend pulled her out. So Tabitha got the money. Time passed by, Tabitha and I got into an argument. I found out that she spent the twelve thousand dollars without giving me my six thousand dollars back. I had also gotten Tabitha a car in my name for her, so the argument got heated. Tabitha told me she wasn't giving me the rest of the money. She did finally gave me my three thousand dollars of it, but she said she was not going to give me the other three thousand dollars. She also said, "I'm not paying on the car any more nor the loan." I got the loan for her on my name. She was making payments on it but stopped all payments.

I never thought my daughter would be so nasty toward me. As I did recall, she would do whatever a man tells her to do. I could hear Winston in the background. I asked Tabitha where was Winston when she needed money. I told Tabitha, "You are always listening to Winston."

And she said, "He doesn't have anything to do with it." Then after I said that I hung up the phone. Tabitha called back and said, "Winston is tired of hearing his name in my mouth." Then I hung up again. Then minutes later I heard a knock on the door.

It was Tabitha coming in yelling, "I'm getting my kids."

I said, "You aren't getting nobody."

Tabitha said to me, "Winston is going to call the police."

I said to Tabitha, "I don't care who he call." So the kids came running down the stairs because Tabitha was trying to get Jay by the hand and pulling him out of the door. So the other child, Jay's older sister, started grabbing him so their mom, Tabitha, could not get him out of the door.

I said, "Leave the children alone. Every time we get into it, you always want to come and get these kids."

Tabitha said to me, "You better let them go. Winston will be calling the police."

I said once again, "I don't care." Finally the police got to my house. I thought I was in the movie *Rush Hour* because when I opened the door, I saw three cop cars. Tabitha and Winston was outside talking to the police, and finally I asked the police to come inside to tell my story.

I told the police that I had raised these children, and that they had been living with me since they were babies while she was doing what she wanted to do and while the fathers were locked up. And I told the officer that Winston just got out of prison. The officer said that he understood but she is their mother. They had to go with her.

So at that time, only three of the kids were home because the other two had school. So the other three had to go with their mom. We had camera around our house. I was in the basement wondering why the police haven't left yet. So I went back upstairs and opened the door and said, "Is there something else?"

The police said, "We're waiting for the other two."

I said, "The other two are at school." If Tabitha knew anything about her kids, she would have known that they were at school. So finally, the police left. Two police cars were at my house.

Chapter 8

Enough is Enough

MY GRANDKIDS HAD TO LEAVE with their mother, Tabitha, when she pulled my grandchildren out of their home. That was when I said ENOUGH IS ENOUGH. I went downstairs and called a lawyer and quit my job. I knew I was headed for war. The kids came back to get some things. I told them, "Everything is going to be okay. Watch the little kids. Make sure they will be alright." I'll never forget that day. My babies were crying and didn't want to get into the car. I walked them out and said, "It will be okay." I looked at Tabitha and said, "I'm my daddy's child."

Tabitha knew what that had meant. Anyone that knew my daddy knows that he was a strong man ready to go to war at any time, did not play about his family. I did not play about my grandchildren. She would drop them off in the morning for school late almost every morning.

Tia had to be to school at 7:40 a.m. She would have to come in and take her bath and put on her uniform and eat. I had to rush to get her to school on time, and Brandon and Janese had time to get to school because they had to be at school at 8:30 a.m. And Raelyn was homeschooled. This went on for about a month. A lot of stress on my grandkids.

Tabitha and Winston would pick them up after school, rushing the kids. I could recall, Janese came in the house. Her clothes were wet. She started wetting herself from all the stress, and I would text the kids every day on and off during the night to make sure they were okay. They would say they're okay, but I could tell they weren't.

Raelyn, the seventeen-year old granddaughter, tried to make sure they were doing alright. I told them to just stick together and look out for one another. I could recall one night, Tabitha and Winston went out to clean an apartment. That was his little business.

The kids called me and said they had nothing to eat. It was 10 o'clock at night. Tabitha finally brought them something to eat. After that, I started making dinner for them to take with them every evening to make sure they would eat every day and pack snacks. My appointment came with the lawyer. My husband and I met with the lawyer.

I got this lady lawyer to represent me. I was still seeing the children every morning and would pick the children up in the evening. This went on for about a month. Finally, Tabitha received the paperwork from the court that I was taking her custody for my grandchildren. Once that happened, she stopped letting me see the kids.

I could recall, Tabitha and Winston said something to my oldest granddaughter, Raelyn, and my granddaughter said something back. Winston got mad and tried to grab his son, Jay. Jay's sister and brother did not let him take Jay. They got between Winston and fussed at him, and Jay's sister, Tia, grabbed him and took him in the house. Winston looked at Tabitha and said, "I don't have time for this shit. Raelyn was not going to talk to me anyway, but she can talk to you however she wants." So Winston threw all their clothes out of the trunk onto the ground and pulled off with their belongings on the ground. So I ran into the house and called the police, and they came and asked what happened.

I told the officer that Winston had thrown their clothes on the ground. The cops said they could not arrest him for that. And before the cops had come, Winston said to Raelyn, "I have something for you bitch." Tabitha didn't say anything, acting as if it was someone else's fault and not hers. It had always been her fault, thinking she can pull these children out this home. She would do anything for a man. Her children never came first. It always was the street, men, and money. She loved these three and wretched people.

So anyhow, once again, the children had to go with their mother. Tabitha said all the children couldn't fit in the car and needed a car seat. So Tabitha and Winston called his sister. I tried to get Tabitha to leave the grandchildren with me until grandpa got off work because we had a van at that time.

Tabitha was talking it over with Winston, her husband who just came out of jail whom she married. The officer came over to tell me that they are talking about it. Tabitha and Winston decided they were going to take the kids with them, and so they did. The cop I was talking to told me to get full custody of those kids, and he was aware of their fathers' criminal records. I told the cop that it was already in process, just waiting for our court dates. I put the kids' clothes back in the bag after Winston had thrown them out onto the ground and into the car. I told Tabitha that she's going to rot in hell for what she had done to these children. So they drove all headed to Reading, Pennsylvania.

Raelyn had texted me and told me that Tabitha was talking about them in front on Winston's sister. I said, "That's okay. Don't worry about it." Finally that night, they made it to Tabitha's house. The children said that if I had not fixed food I had sent with them, they would not have eaten that night. So I told the kids good night, and I'll see them in the morning.

The process had started. I had to attend this class for grandparents and parents who were seeking custody for their children and grandchildren. I had to go to mediation with Tabitha. I never knew my daughter was a big liar until then. She told lies on me and her children to make herself and her husband look good.

But the mediation lady could see right through her. After that, I would be worn out and drained from all the lies I was hearing. Time to go to mediation again. I told the Lord, "I'm tired. I don't want to be bothered with Tabitha and her husband." It got so bad. I had to end it early because Tabitha allowed her husband, Winston, to say things against my grandchildren that wasn't true. Drained once again. This case was moving fast. I had one more mediation to go to with my lawyer. We were there, but there was no Tabitha nor Winston. They did not show up, and the lady said that we were going to continue on.

Everyone got their paperwork, and I'll send it down to the judge. I should have no problem with the judge signing off on this.

I received the paperwork in the mail. It stated that I had full custody of my grandchildren. I said, "Thank you, God."

The next day, my daughter had called me and said, "Do we have court?"

I said, "We had court Thursday." Tabitha thought court was Friday.

She asked me, "What did the mediation say? I told her that we would receive the order in the mail and we did. I also ended up calling Winston's PO Officer to tell him that he came to my home and threw all the kids' clothes.

The PO stated that he had spoken with Winston and stated that he could not talk on what they had talked about because of confidentiality. So time had passed on. Tabitha and Winston started a basketball team, and my grandkids were on that team. They liked playing on the team but did not like the ghetto people that would be around them.

Winston's sister and Raelyn got into an argument because Winston's sister was messing around with Jay. Being the oldest, you were taught to take up for your sisters and brothers. Winston's sister was all up in Raelyn's face. Mind you, she's a grown-up woman in her thirties, and Raelyn was sixteen at that time.

So Raelyn was giving her mouth back about her brother, and Tabitha told Winston's sister, "My kid and you, don't be up in her face." Everything calmed down, and when Raelyn got home, she told me about what had happened. And Tabitha said that Winston's sister was bothering Jay and called him a cry baby and pulling on him, and Raelyn stepped in and told her to stop bothering her brother.

From that, Winston's sister got loud, and that's when Tabitha said, "You can chill with all that because that's my child." I was surprised Tabitha took up for Raelyn because when the children was taken from me, Raelyn said that they were over Winston's sister's house. And Tabitha was talking about her and her other sister and said that they were troublemakers. And when they got to Tabitha's house, Tabitha and Winston got into an argument, and Winston left.

So Tabitha called her girl friends over to comfort her, and while they were there, Brandon heard Tabitha called Raelyn and Tia a bitch while talking to her friends. Not only that, it was getting late and Tabitha had not fed the children. The children remembered I had made dinner for them. So Tia warmed up the food and fed her brothers and sisters. Tia was being their mother. There was a time Tia had to cook for them because Tabitha was too busy being in the bedroom with Winston and did not interact with the children while they were with her.

They would always go to the attic and be with each other. I would always text to see how things were going. They said they were tired of being in the attic because they had nothing to do. Tabitha had a TV in the attic, but there was not much to watch because it didn't work, only games. The children became bored, and the little ones would argue all the time because the older girls would call and tell me what would be going on.

I would say, "Try to keep the little ones entertained." So the next morning, they would get dropped off by my house to go to school. They would look a mess. The little one Jay would not have shoes on, just socks, and he had asthma. He would not be properly dressed for winter. The older girls had to get the little ones ready every morning for a month. This went on while Tabitha would lay in bed most of the time.

Winston would bring them to Grandma's house, and Tia would always be late for school. And it went on and on. It was stressing the children out. Tabitha did not care about her own children. She treated Winston like he was a child and my grandchildren like they were grown-ups. They had to do everything for themselves. My oldest granddaughter, Raelyn, had called the police and told them.

There was a knock at the door, and Tabitha said, "Is there a problem?"

And the police said, "We got a call from their papa that there was a fight between you and your husband Winston."

Tabitha said, "I don't know what you're talking about."

Then Tabitha's friends were there and said, "We didn't hear any noise." So Raelyn told the police how Tabitha had been treating them.

And Tabitha said, "I took them from their grandmother, and they are trying to get back to her." The police went on his way, went out one ear to the other. In other words, he believed Tabitha. I never knew that my daughter would treat her own children this way, but again, I could believe she had never put them first.

She hardly ever told them she loves them. But every time she turned around, she would always tell her boyfriend "I love you" about three or four times a day. Or when she would come by and see the children, walking in the house on the phone and leaving out on the phone, never hanging up. So I told her, "You're always on that phone. You never talk to these kids."

Raelyn told me that when she was at her mother's house, Jay would be sick, and she had to take care of him and give him a breathing treatment because Mom would be in the room with Winston. This was affecting Tia's grades. She had gotten an F on a subject. Yes, she had an F before and always had a chance to make it up. But at this time, she was at Tabitha's house. Tabitha wasn't helping with homework.

She would not ask if they had homework. The oldest girl had to help the little ones with their work, and that's how Tia ended up with a D. But she did pass onto her next grade. Thank God for that. The oldest kids continued to watch out for their brother and sister. They had to clean. Tabitha had never kept a clean house, and her husband Winston said that they had dirtied it up. But I had the children to take pictures of the house. It was not even fit to live in. She only had one bedroom, and the children had the attic.

The bunk beds were weak, and the children had only a sheet on the bed. So I went to the Dollar General to buy them new sheets and covers because they said at nighttime, they would be cold and also bought food because they would be hungry. So I started making dinner every evening to take with them since Tabitha wasn't making anything. They had to take care of themselves. All Tabitha cared about was being laid up next to Winston.

She did not care about the children missing me. My grandson Brandon beg her at one time to let them see me. Tabitha told the youngest child, "You're never going to see your grandmother again." As you know, that wasn't true. I was awarded custody of all five of my grandchildren. I could not have done this on my own. It was because of God

45

that fought for me. He had a plan for me. I went out and got letters from businesses that knew me in the community, just names a few of the stores that knew me and my grandchildren since they were babies.

I got to know managers of these stores, and they had gotten to know us. Some of the stores are Walmart, Dollar General, and Boscov's. These people wrote letters on my behalf, and family, and friends. I had a friend that gave me money toward my lawyer, and she gave me money because I wasn't working. These children had been my life.

I had always looked after them and their grandfather. I would go and get them if Tabitha had dropped them off to places they should not be. I knew this was war. I could not allow Tabitha to continue to take these children out of their home, the stable home they ever knew. My grandchildren and I had been together. I would take them down South with me every summer to see their great-grandmother.

I started out with Raelyn. We would fly every summer, and then came along Tia; we would head down South, and then came Brandon. My circle got bigger and bigger. But I did not mind, and then came Janese, more fun. And then came baby Jay. I no longer could fly because it got expensive. Then we began to ride the train. Jay was just a baby riding on the train with Grandma. It was hard for me with a newborn baby.

But I did it because I'm a strong person, and it would be the first time to see his great-grandma. There was a lady on the train who offered to help me with Jay. He was crying, so she took the little ones and walked them back and forth down the aisle. And Jay had calmed down, and finally he went to sleep. I'm glad he did. I wasn't able to sleep because I was holding him. It was so uncomfortable that I did not get too much rest because I was keeping my eyes on the other children while they slept. This trip continued. My oldest grandchild is seventeen, and that was how long I have been going back to the South to see my mom. All these years until this day, we still make the trip by car, train, and plane.

But we always managed to get there. My daughter had taken us to down South several times. We always had a good time when we are traveling. We would sing to songs on the radio. We would go live on Facebook, and the children would be dancing from the backseat. We would have fun, stop at the rest stop area, and get out to stretch our legs, and talk to other people. They would ask where we're headed, and the kids would always say, "I'm going to see my grandma."

One summer when I went to visit my mom, I met my first cousin for the first time from Buffalo, New York. She said to me, "I admire you."

Traveling on a train with small children, only three others were small. The other big kids help with the little kids. We would always travel, so they knew the routine, and my brother from Atlanta would always be there to pick us up at the train station. He was so impressed how the children all had something in their hands.

That's called helping out. He was impressed. He told his wife about it when he got home. I could recall when the kids and I were going through this custody battle. They would call me, but most of all, we would text. I could recall, Raelyn calling me crying because Mother Tabitha had her to take care of the little ones.

Raelyn had to bathe the little ones at night while she would be in her room with Winston with the door closed. Raelyn was sixteen at that time. It's a lot for a sixteen-year old when you have to take care of four siblings while Tabitha do nothing but stay on the phone and under a grown man like a child or handicapped. From this day, I resent my daughter on how she treated my grandchildren. Still until this day, I have no respect for someone who had mistreated her children for a man. It's because she doesn't love herself, can only love a man. Something in that small brain of her cannot relate to love her children. The Bible says that children are a blessing to you.

My grandchildren had been a blessing to me, but not my own daughter. She never apologized for how she treated me, her dad, nor her children. She will never have a place in my heart until she makes up and apologizes to me and the children and her dad. It will remain the same. Tabitha calls the kids sometimes, not much. She doesn't visit at all unless she brings money by, and that doesn't happen often.

Did I tell you Tabitha is having another baby? Tabitha will be having a boy. I'm going to guess how this is going to work out because she had never raised the five children she had. Tabitha was not just cut out to be a mother.

I have never thought my daughter would turn out to be the person that she had become—the love of money and man. I call it the two-man and money. That's what makes her happy. Her children could never have a place in her heart until she looks at what kind of person she had become. That's why you should be careful who you hang around. If you hang out with trash you will become trash.

People that tell you the wrong things. People that think for you. People that order you around. Tabitha always would follow the crowd and never went with her own mind. She always wants to impress people that didn't have anything.

Tabitha grew up in a house, had nice parents, nice clothes, but somehow she wants to hang out with ghetto people. They would just blow her mind, the things they taught her—how to lie and much more. She would go to the dangerous places. After a while, she became them and talked like them.

Lost all respect for herself and her mother and father and her children. The world turned her upside down as a child, and now that she in her thirties, remains that child today. I pray for Tabitha that she will find her way back to God and her parents but most of all her children.

I would always say to Tabitha when we did talk one day, "You are going to need these children, and they want nothing to do with you." And that's how it is today. The children don't care if they ever see her again, remembering how they were treated that month they had to live with her.

I would tell the children, "Hold on. Everything's going to be okay. Grandma got a lawyer. Just hang in there." The little one named Jay, who was four, sometimes asks about mom but not much.

We had moved on with our lives, but Tabitha was having a hard time moving on. I say that because sometimes she would call me talk junk about things she has no control of. Tabitha was fine with me when I didn't have custody. Now that I have paperwork on them, she doesn't like it. Tabitha likes it when I had to get permission to take them to the doctors, permission to check them out of school. She loved it when I had to answer to her, but now she doesn't like to answer to me she calling, starting stuff with me. I had to tell Tabitha,

"I have custody of these children now. You cannot do what you want anymore." Tabitha never did anything much anyway.

The only time Tabitha would do something for these kids would be their birthday and Christmas. Sometimes she would bring some money but not much. She barely would come and see the children, but when her boyfriends would get out, then she would play like she was interested in the children. But when they are locked up, she doesn't come around. My daughter will never become the mother to these children because it's too late and because still to this day, 2017 and 2018, she had not apologized and did not come and see them.

I am ashamed of my daughter because I brought her up to be respectful to herself and others. Tabitha was brought up in the church. My husband's cousin had lived in the same complex as Tabitha and told my husband that she believed Tabitha had become a Muslim. She did not tell us. We heard it from other people off the streets. No one would tell me because they knew no matter what, I did not allow anyone to speak bad about my children. Tabitha had come by the house one day, and I saw it for myself.

I didn't say a word, "If that's what you want to do, that's on you." Almost all of the boyfriends she had, were Muslim and drug dealers, always in and out of prison. Tabitha would go and visit them put money on their book while my husband and I bought everything they need. Don't get me wrong. I love buying things for my grandkids.

The point that I'm making is that the money should have gone to my grandchildren. She would buy her boyfriend's clothes and sneakers and would give money to put in their pockets and credit card. Tabitha bought her last boyfriend a car, who is now Tabitha's husband. I could recall Tabitha coming by the house to pick us up to go get our hair done. We all were just talking in the car, and Tabitha said something to Raelyn. And Raelyn said something back to Tabitha, and all hell broke loose. Raelyn told her mother, "You've never been there for us, grandma has." Why did Raelyn say that?

Tabitha turned around to hit Raelyn who was in the back, reached her arm to the back seat trying to hit Raelyn for what she had said. I told Tabitha, "Take us back home. We're not riding with you before you kill us all or yourself trying to fight your daughter. Take us back home now." So Tabitha took us back. This was not the only time Tabitha had tried to fight Raelyn.

Once, I was on the phone with Tabitha. I can't remember what it was about, but Tabitha got into her car from where she lived. It wasn't around the comer. I could hear her boyfriend say, "I would not let Raelyn talk to me like that."

So there was a knock at the door. It was Tabitha. I told Raelyn to go to her room and lock the door and don't come down. You know kids, they don't listen. So Raelyn came down, and I was keeping them apart, and Tabitha broke loose from me and started fighting Raelyn. Raelyn was giving it to her. Raelyn was fighting her back, and all Raelyn's sisters and brothers started fighting Tabitha. Finally, I got Tabitha off of Raelyn and told her what kind of mother fights their child.

One thing about Tabitha, she likes when someone gets her hype, never listens to the right thing. Like I said before, she likes that thug life. I have tried to talk to Tabitha about her children telling her that one day she's going to need these kids to bring her a glass of water, and they're not going to have anything to do with her. As it is now, they don't want to see her nor talk to her. The kids lost all trust and love for their mother. These children are my life. They make grandma happy, and I'll go to the moon and back for them. They are my world. Every morning when they come into my room and say, "Good morning, Grandma."

I would reply, "Good morning," back. I just smile from cheek to cheek.

The Aftermath

I have good respectful grandchildren. I'm not saying that because they are mine, but they work hard. Raelyn is seventeen years old. She works, have good grades, and does homeschool. Tia who is thirteen years old and also being homeschooled, also had good grades. Brandon who is homeschooled also have good grades and also plays basketball and takes swimming classes and likes to play the Xbox One. Janese, who is a very good girl, is homeschooled and makes good grades and also takes swimming classes and always on her tablet playing Skate Universal and also always dances.

Jay, who is four years old, goes to school. He is in pre-kindergarten. He does very well in school and is also in swimming classes. He likes to play on the Xbox One and basketball. All are great grandchildren to have. They taught grandma how to text, how to get on YouTube. If I don't know how to do something, they all come and say "Grandma, we can help you."

Well in Alabama, I had to talk to the judge about one of the father who wants his mother to be able to see his daughter which is her granddaughter. She wanted to be able to see her so the court awarded her once a month to see her grandchild because when I was allowing her to come to my house, she would bring other people with her without my permission, and I got tired of that. People have no respect for your home or have enough respect to ask if they could bring someone else to your home.

I'm a private person. I do not allow anyone to come into my home, so I had to tell her and her son that they weren't allowed to come here anymore. That's why the person was seeking from the court that she be given rights to see her granddaughter. She comes once a month to pick her up at my house, only if the court says it's okay from me, and that's fine because I know she won't take up my time. The only time and dates are set up between Tabitha who is Janese's mother. I have no contact with the mother. She comes by and picks Janese up, and I send Janese out the door.

I had to fuss with other grandparents, father, sisters, and mothers concerning my grandkids. They always want to tell me what to do, but my husband and I are the only ones that took them all into, making sure they remain together.

Chapter 9

My Journey with God

I CAN'T FIGURE OUT WHY it took me so long to file for custody for my grandchildren, but God knew why God works everything out for me. Through God I had strength for favorable help. God had a plan. At first I did not see it. God began to show me little by little through this program on Facebook every morning. She would come on at 5:55 A.M., and as I was going through this custody battle, God had a hearty word for me each morning.

I began to see that I was going to be all right and so were the kids. Every morning, I would listen to her word for the day. I would meditate on the word day and night. I knew I was getting ready to face a battle. I would listen to the teacher over and over that was on Facebook on April 12, 2017. I found out why I was listening to the seven messages. It was because God was getting me ready for my battle as I said before on April 12, 2017.

My daughter had been arguing on the phone about money. I had given her to start her business and did not want to pay it back. I found out she spent the whole twelve thousand dollars to herself, so I hung up the phone. And that day, my life changed and my grandchildren's life changed. Also, Tabitha and her boyfriend called the cops and had my grandchildren removed out of the house. That's when my battle began.

I called the lawyer as I had stated earlier in the book. I did all that I had to do, go to classes, go to mediation, but God had a plan for me. And it was on each morning through this lady on Facebook that came on every morning, so I began to get my message each morning on January 19, 2017.

God began to give me my message through this lady on Facebook. My first message was "Giants do fall for" (Samuel 17:8–11). God was letting me know that he will defeat my enemies. God will deliver me from giants. My giants were Tabitha and Winston. God also wanted me to know God will fight my battles. It's by God's power in me that he will defeat my enemies, no matter how big my problems are. I must say I had a big problem. God was telling me, "Don't run from your enemies."

God said, "I got you."

God also said, "Be ready to fight your giants because giants fall in the name of Jesus."

God wanted me to rely on him and have faith. Don't run. God will see you through. God wanted me to depend on him, and I did. But there were times I was like God. *Come on. I need you. Look, I'm getting beaten up over here.* It seems as if God wasn't there on January 24, 2017. God had a message through the lady on Facebook, the title was "Cause my enemies to slumber first" (Samuel 1:26). God was telling me that he is my battle fighter, and God wants me to wait on him and trust him that everything will fall into place, and God wanted me to know that he protects my grandchildren and me. And God will put our enemies to sleep, and God will cause your enemies to be so busy that they don't know one day from another.

As you could recall, I told you Tabitha had called me on a Friday and said, "Do we have court?"

I said that we had court on Thursday. If that's what God meant about "cause your enemies to slumber," just wondering. We had court on Thursday evening and asked me, "Don't we have court?

I said, "We had court today which was Thursday Tabitha."

We had court on Thursday and she went on to ask me, "What did the mediation say?" The mediation said that we will receive the paperwork in the mail from the court. The court will make the decision, so I received the paperwork and got custody off all five of my grandchildren. That was the best day of my life, having all my grandchildren back with me. I don't know if she was sleeping or too busy that she forgot her court date, but she did. And God also wanted me to know that he will bring his promise to pass, and God wanted me to know that he will bless me and my grandchildren through seen and unseen danger. And he did that whatever they had plot. The lies they had told, it did not work because God had my plan written out. And the next morning, I woke up with a message from the lady on Facebook, inside was "Enough is enough" on March 16, 2017. God was telling me, "Whatever comes your way, I will step in."

God was letting me know through this message, "I got you. You don't have to be afraid. I got your back?" He wants me to know that I don't have to be. When my daughter, Tabitha, received the paperwork that I was taking her to court for custody for all of five of my grandchildren, she had brought them back. But when she found out I was taking her to court, she took them back to her house. I stayed in contact with them every day and even Tabitha and Winston.

Came to pick the oldest granddaughter up because she was homeschooled. She got into an argument with Tabitha's husband once, and I told you the story about him who threw the clothes out of the car. And the kids had to call the cops when that wasn't even the case once and was doing it for himself.

God had made my path plain from a lady on Facebook who knew nothing about me nor I knew nothing about her, but God used her each day to give me a message. And God went on to say, "I have seen what have been happening to you and what have been done to you." He wants me to know that he was stepping in to protect my grandchildren.

God said in his word, "Vegeance is mine," and God used that lady to speak to me by saying to me not to rush the process because he was with me and my grandchildren on April 12, 2017.

I knew what is enough is enough. That is the day they came and took my grandchildren. Tabitha called the cops, and my babies were removed. But on April 17, I received, "Worry not, I got you." I got up early each morning for a month listening to this lady whom I have passed through her page before, never really interested in her until now.

I decided to listen to her, and I began to listen to her every morning. After that moment and at that moment, she had another message that she spoke on the title. It was "The Lord is sending you help." And God did. Yes, that he had people to help by writing letters on my behalf, gave me money to help pay my lawyer.

God wanted me to know that his hand was in it, and that he was moving on my behalf. My enemies want to destroy me. I need Tabitha and Winston, my grandchildren's mom and one of my grandchild's father, but God will send the help you need. Sometimes we have to wait for him. Don't get me wrong. It is hard to wait, but I had to wait and pray. The next morning, I got up. There was another message for me on May 1, 2017.

"God is making a way for you" coming from Esther 1 to 5 and 10 to 12. God wanted me to know hell or high water. God wanted me to trust him through it all. God wanted me to know that he will make a way for his people. God wanted me to know that his plan will come to pass for us. Also, he wanted me to know that he will change the way things should go, so the way can be made for me and my grandchildren. God will alter things for you and me, and he did and all confusion I went through.

God wanted me to know that he would be there for me, and he was there. It wasn't easy. I need God to make way for me. I had to listen to lies after lies, but God was still there with me. He gave me the strength to go and do what I had to do for my two grandchildren, and that was to tell the truth about Tabitha. I had another message on May 15, 2017: God is fighting for you (Esther 6:11–14).

God was telling me, "Don't be afraid over evildoers." My evildoers were Tabitha and Winston. God said that he will fight my battles for me, and when I say he will fight my battle, he will. He had the right people in my path, praying people to call me and said that they would help in any way. And they would call and check on the custody case just like Haman trying to destroy Mordecai. God the Father was with his battles and defeated his enemies just like God defeated my enemies Tabitha and Winston.

God turned everything around in my favor. You could tell when God is fighting for you but remember you still have to go through your battle, and also you have to fight for yourself. I did that by getting a lawyer, getting statement on my behalf, praying, fasting.

That means doing the necessary things you have to do to win. Don't forget, you can't win without God. I realized at that moment, there's nothing too hard for God. I have always realized that God can make a way out of no way.

He did it for me. He could do it for you. In the last message was "God will lift you." I could not find the date on this message. No matter, it's just God letting you know that no matter what you go through, he will be with you, and he will lift you out of your problems. And he did. God gave me five beautiful grandchildren. All that my family and I went through, it was time for us to go on our summer vacation. We would fly down South to see my mom who is their great-grandmother. We also went to their favorite place in Atlanta called Stars and Strikes. My husband and I went to the Bahamas for five days. I needed this vacation. I was tired mentally and physically of all the fighting, physical fighting but just worn out by the lies.

So the first day, my husband and I met our friends in Orlando, Florida, our military friends who we haven't seen in a long time. It was three couples, good friends getting away to have fun. When we finally got on board, the DJ was playing music, getting you ready to party.

We want to play casino. We went to see a comedy show. We took pictures. We took walks around the ship to see the beautiful rooms they had on the boat. They had a raffle in the jewelry store. We listened to the piano in the bar area, and the last night, we took pictures and had dinner with everyone on the boat.

Also, we went to the beach with our friends, went to breakfast with our friends. There's so much food to eat until you did not know where to begin, desserts which I'd never seen before. My husband really spoiled me. He has been a wonderful man for thirty years and said that I need a well-rested vacation after what I had been through. I wrote this book to tell all grandparents.

Chapter 10

They Were Worth Fighting For

IF YOU ARE SEEKING CUSTODY of them, if you know that they are not being taken care of or being in danger, do whatever you have to do. Keep them safe. I don't care if you have to sell chicken dinner or raise funds in GoFundMe page or borrow the money from the bank. Whatever it takes, please keep these children safe. My husband and I went through my bank account and had to borrow money from his 401k and had a friend that helped us with our lawyer

I say once again, do what you have to do. If you do, God will make a way for you like if it not had been for the Lord showing me this lady page on Facebook and had my plan mapped out for me, I would not had won the fight with our God's guidance. Thank you, Lord, for giving me my grandchildren back to me.

I called them my babies, and also, I went on a forty-day fast while doing the custody hearing because the lady on Facebook said, "If you need God to do something for you, you need to go on this fast." At the time, I felt that I needed to do this fast.

I told my niece to go on it with me, and she did. At the time, I do not know why he didn't mean I'm a witness to that. It wasn't easy, but I made it through God's strength, friends, and family. I can do it. I just got started. I salute all the grandparents that have raised their grandchildren. I salute you again, and I dedicate this book to all grandparents who have a raised their grandchildren.

The reason why I named my book *Enough Is Enough* is because my daughter had done a lot of things to me, to her children, and her dad. But I knew on April 12, 2017, when the cops took my grand-children away, I knew then that I had enough of Tabitha's mess. And I wasn't going to take it anymore. I got the title from the lady's message "Enough is enough." The reason why I'm writing this book is because I want grandparents that are raising their grandchildren that it's not right for parents to just pull the kids out of their home while being raised as babies and still in your home at the ages of two, four, nine, thirteen, and seventeen years old.

It just isn't right to raise a child that long, and parents feel that it's okay. Just because things are not going their way. I would also like to say to all the single moms that take excellent care of their children to keep up the good work. I know it isn't easy. I myself was a single mom. I took care of my two children with help from my mom. But I raised my children, and so can you. Today, lots of single moms put their men first. That's not how it should be. Your children should come first. They need their mother. Women put men first that have criminal records, hardly know them, and bring them near their kid's life.

Protect your children. Love them, and cherish them. Tabitha never protected her children. She always protected her boyfriends. She lied for them. She had taken a case for one of them. Her investments were never on her kids. I never dreamt that I would have raised a daughter like Tabitha.

She turned out to be a mean, nasty, a lover of the world. I can truly say that one day I pray that she will come back to Jesus. Until that day, she will keep working for the devil. You raise these children, and parents feel that they can come and take them any time they want. You get up with them when they are babies to feed them or change them or hold these children when they are afraid. Where is Mommy and Daddy? You take them to school in the winter-freezing cold. The child hadn't even been taken care of by the parents when the mom get food stamps and let her friends use them before she gives them to the grandparents whom have been taking care of them.

I could not have made it without these scriptures
God is fighting for you (Esther 6:11–14)
The end.

I could not have made it without these scriptures:

God is fighting for you (Esther 6:11-14)

God was telling me not to fret over evildoers. God said that he will fight my battle for me and when I say he will fight your battle, he will. He had the right people in my path, people were praying. He had some call me and they said that they would help me pay my lawyer. People would call and check on me. Everyone I saw in the street was speaking they are praying for me. Just like God turned everything around in my favor, you can tell when God is fighting for you. God will fight for you, but you still have to go through your battle and also you have to fight for yourself. That means doing the necessary things you have to do to win. Don't forget, you can't win without God and I realize at that moment there's nothing too hard for God.

God is making a way for you (Esther 1-5, 10-12)

Come hell or high water we are going to trust you. You make a way for your people. When God has a plan for us, it will come to pass. He will change the way things should go so that the method can be made for you; God will alter things for you. We have to know that God will make in confusion.

The Lord is sending you help.

God will send people to help you. We can see God's hand moving. The enemies come to destroy you, but God will send the help you need. Just wait on him.

Enough is Enough 2 Samuel 24:10-17

God is stepping in for the thing that could come your way. Enough is Enough. God said, I got you, I got your back. You don't have to worry anymore. I will vindicate you. I will lift you up. I stood in faith believing. I see what have been doing to you. I'm stepping in. I protect my children. Vengeance is mine. Don't rush your process. That's enough she has been faithful God is saying.

Cause my enemies to slumber 1 Samuel 1:26

God you did it last time and you will do it again. I'm not going to take the matter into my hands. I release it unto you. God is our battle fighter. Wait on God and trusts him. Everything will fall into place.

God protects us and will put our enemies to sleep. God will cause your enemies to stay so busy that they don't know one day from another. God is with you. He will bring your promise to pass. God will bless you through seen and unseen danger.

Giants do fall 1 Samuel 17:8-11

God will deliver you from your giants. God will fight your battle. It is by God power and might that he will defeat your enemies. No matter how big the problem is, don't run from it. God got you. Be ready to fight your giants. Giants do fall in the name of Jesus. Rely on God. Have faith; don't. run. See it through. Whatever you may be going through depend on God.

Your enemies are defeated. When people do you dirty God will fight your enemies. God gives us victory over our enemies even when it looks like they might be winning.

God will lift you.

God will lift you out of your problems.

God is coming to your rescue.

God will deliver us out of our problems. Just trust him. When you don't see him moving just know God has already worked it out.

About the Author

THE AUTHOR IS A WIFE and is married for over thirty years, a mother, and dedicated grandmother who wanted to share her love for her grandchildren and motivation to fight for them.

CPSIA information can be obtained
at www.ICGtesting.com
Printed in the USA
LVHW111251080319
609982LV00001B/67/P

9 781640 961654